ONE SPECTACULAR DAY

Sam's Spectacular Day at School

Robin Coale

To order additional copies of this book, contact:
Xlibris
1-888-795-4274
www.Xlibris.com
Orders@Xlibris.com

ISBN: Softcover   978-1-7960-6683-8
       Hardcover   978-1-7960-6684-5
       EBook   978-1-7960-6682-1

Print information available on the last page

Rev. date: 10/23/2019

Inspired by Mae Williams, who taught me

everyone can have an

EXTRAORDINARY VOCABULARY!

Love, Aunt Robin

XO XO

Sam woke up slowly this morning, and in a

somnambulistic

state wondered, "Am I dreaming or am I awake?"

(som-**nam**-by*uh*-lis-tik = like sleepwalking, half awake)

Mom **bellowed** from the kitchen,
"Time to get up and get ready for school!"

(**bel**-oh = to roar)

Sam rolled out of bed from a prone

position to upright, thinking,

(**prohn** = lying flat, face down)

(**uhp**-rīt = sitting up)

"Today I'm going to have a positive mental attitude."

(a **positive mental attitude** is looking for the good in things, optimistic, and hopeful)

"I'm coming, Mom," Sam shouted, while

changing into school apparel.

(uh-**par**-uhl = clothes)

Sam skipped to the kitchen and **situated comfortably** at the counter, announcing,

"Today is going to be a **spectacular** day!"

(**sich**-oo-ā-tid = located or placed in a certain position)

(**kuhm**-fer-t*uh*-b*uh*-lee = in a way that feels relaxed (good))

(spek-**tak**-yuh-ler = fabulous, fantastic (really great))

After **consuming** breakfast,

Sam waited out front for the school bus to arrive.

(kuhn-**soom**-ng = eating up)

Boarding the bus, the driver asked Sam to go to the back.

"May I **negotiate** a seat in the front?" asked Sam.

They settled on a **compromise**, and Sam sat by the window two seats back.

(**bohr**-ding = getting up into)

(ni-**goh**-shee-āt = to make a deal, work it out)

(**kom**-pr*uh*-mīz = settle your differences, agree, understand)

At school, Sam was **determined** to **succeed** in **arithmetic**.

"I like **mathematics**!" Sam **exclaimed**.

(dih-**tur**-mind = decided, wholly (*for sure*))

(s*uh*k-**seed** = to work out)

(*uh*-**rith**-m*uh*-tik = studying (learning about) numbers)

(math-*uh*-**mat**-iks = working with numbers, figures and forms, math)

(eks-**klām** = to speak out, as in surprise or excitement)

"Addition, subtraction, multiplication, and division. Calculating is fun!"

(*uh*-**dish**-*uh*n = adding together)

(s*uh*b-**trak**-*shuh*n = taking away (minus))

(muhl-t*uh*-pli-**kā**-sh*uh*n = making many (times))

(dih-**vizh**-*uh*n = separating into parts)

(**kal**-ky*uh*-lā-ting = doing math)

During recess, several of Sam's classmates were involved in an exciting soccer competition.

Sam built up the confidence to ask, "May I participate?"

The children welcomed another teammate.

(**sev**-er-*uh*l = more than two)

(kom-pi-**tish**-*uh*n = a contest)

(**kon**-fi-d*uh*ns = full trust, belief) (self-confidence is belief in yourself, belief that "you can do it")

(pahr-**tis**-*uh*-pāt = to share with others)

(**wel**-*kuh*md = greeted kindly)

Running, kicking, and passing were

exhilarating!

(eg-**zil**-*uh*-rā-ting = a feeling of being very happy)

That evening at dinner, while eating a

delectable meal,

Mom asked Sam, "How was your day?"

(dih-**lek**-t*uh*-b*uh*l = enjoyable, delicious)

Sam announced, "It was **one SPECTACULAR day!!**"

(spek-**tak**-yuh-ler = fabulous, fantastic (really great))

Printed in the United States
By Bookmasters